RYAN GIGGS

HEROES

First published in 1997 by
Invincible Press
an imprint of HarperCollins*Publishers*
London

© The Foundry Creative Media Company Ltd 1997 (text)

A CIP catalogue record for this book is available from the British Library.

ISBN 0 00 218819 8

Created and produced by Flame Tree Publishing, a part of
The Foundry Creative Media Company Ltd,
The Long House, Antrobus Road,
Chiswick, London W4 5HY.

RYAN GIGGS

HEROES

Introduction and main text by
Alex Wilkins

RYAN GIGGS started his career by being constantly compared to George Best. There *were* similarities: both wore a number 11 shirt, were skilled wingers and were denied the opportunity of performing on a European Stage with their respective international sides. But Ryan has since created his own legend. A forward who enjoys flying down the left flank, skipping past bewildered defenders and scoring goals, Giggsy is a professional who loves the thrill of the chase and turning a defensive move into an attacking one. His manager, Alex Ferguson, can't praise him enough: *His ability is heaven sent, a footballer of his calibre pops up maybe once in a couple of generations.* Who else could he be describing but Ryan Giggs?

Giggs signed as a professional for Manchester United on his 17th birthday – 29 November 1990. Few players have made as stunning a debut: May 1991, during an emotional derby match against old rivals Manchester City, when Giggs scored the only goal in front of a cheering Old Trafford crowd.

During the 1991-92 season, Giggs found himself competing for positions with the flying Ukrainian Andrei Kanchelskis and the PFA Young Player of the Year Lee Sharpe. However, Giggsy soon claimed the PFA trophy for himself when he won the Young Player of the Year Award at the end of the year – his first full season as a professional.

United's win in the Rumbelows Cup in February 1992 saw the first of Ryan's medals, followed by Giggs catapulting United into the League Cup Final when he scored an extra-time winner against Middlesbrough in the second leg of the semi-final. After such victory, beating Nottingham Forest was a mere formality for the 19 year old.

Only a month later, Giggs notched up more medals as part of the winning side in the FA Youth Cup Final, second leg, against Crystal Palace. A game won 3-2 at Old Trafford and 6-3 on aggregate.

Though Giggs scored only nine goals during the 1992-93 season, he was included in the last home match of the season. United had already won the title, but Blackburn had taken an early lead, trying to spoil the Champions' party. Inevitably, Giggs scored the equaliser in front of the partisan 40,000 crowd.

1993 was a year of accolades: Giggs made his first international debut for Wales, against Belgium, and was awarded the PFA Young Player of the Year award for the second time in three years. As a result, critics suggested that he'd peaked at the ripe old age of 20, but Giggs proved them wrong again when, during the 1995-96 season he was back at the top of his game. Alongside Eric Cantona, his team play blossomed, and Giggsy claimed another FA Cup Winners' Medal after United beat Liverpool in the dying minutes of the game.

It could have been different for the young Giggs. He was once selected for the England Youth Team as a substitute, but when called on to the pitch, he took so long warming-up that the match had finished before he came on. Had he done so, he could have been an England, rather than a Welsh, player. England selectors will rue their omission for years to come...

Giggs can still display moments of self-doubt but, as he showed during United's match against Juventus (the team's European campaign in 1996-97), no one can match him. Storming down the wing, breaking down the defence, Giggs dazzled everyone on the European stage.

Giggs has matured and now he's coming into the prime of his career and fulfilling the star status that supporters from the North to the South can all recognise.

Alex Wilkins

STARTING OUT

RYAN GIGGS (OR RYAN WILSON as he was then known) was born in the Welsh capital, Cardiff, on 19 November 1973. He grew up kicking a football around the backyard but, with Danny Wilson, a keen Rugby League player for a father, Ryan was equally at home with a rugby ball.

In 1981, the family moved to Swinton as Danny had been offered professional terms with Swinton Rugby League Club. It was here that Giggs's football career really started.

Giggs started playing football in his local school team, Grosvenor Road Primary, and his talent was quickly spotted by Dennis Schofield, a scout for Manchester City. Schofield recommended him to Dean's, a youth football club, in Salford. Ryan's career didn't get off to a flying start – his team lost 9-1 in his first match. Even so, Giggs was still impressive.

I was transfixed by the little lad. The way he was going down the left wing was like a professional – he was brilliant.
Dennis Schofield, scout for Manchester City

*He was outstanding,
a different class to
the rest of us and
exceptionally quick.
We knew that if we
got the ball to Ryan,
we'd have a chance
to score.*
A former Deans team-mate

GIGGS THEN had a trial with Salford Juniors. He played well and though he was put into the B team, his side won 8-1 – Ryan had scored 6 of the goals. He was never picked for the B team at Salford again. When Giggs was 12, Schofield suggested that he start training at City's Centre of Excellence where he was given the chance to work on his skills and team up with other promising young footballers. His love of United was obvious even there – he often turned up to work out at City wearing a red T-shirt, even though they were banned from the training ground.

This training gave him the chance to show what he was capable of. When Ryan was 14, the Salford Juniors Under-16 team made it to the national final against St. Helens at Old Trafford. Although his team lost, the match gave Giggs a taste of playing inside the Manchester United stadium and he realised that he wanted to be back there, only this time as a professional footballer.

What Giggs can do with the ball has been making seasoned professional watchers react as uninhibitedly as fans ever since he was discreetly lured away from Manchester City's School of Excellence to play a trial for United.
Hugh McIlvanney, *The Sunday Times*, 12 December 1993

I was almost in tears watching him perform.
Alan Smith, Organiser of the Greater Manchester County Schools Under-15 team

AS A YOUNG teenager playing for the Salford Boys against a team of trialists from United, Giggs scored three goals in a match whose final result was 4-3 – his team won. Ryan's talent may not have made him particularly popular with the losing side of other potential United players but Giggs had woven his magic and United were hooked.

*As soon as I saw him on the pitch,
I knew he was a special footballer.
We set out to make him a Manchester
United player.*
Alex Ferguson, manager of Manchester United

Thank God we got him.
Bobby Charlton

*His pace, his balance, his general
football knowledge, the way he
caressed the ball and his shooting.
He had everything.*
**Harold Wood, one of the chief
stewards at Manchester United**

HAD HE NOT been snapped up by
United, Giggs might never have become
a footballer. As a teenager, he showed a
great aptitude for Rugby League and
played for the Salford Boys' team. They
had regular tough matches against
their rivals St Helens, Wigan and
Widnes with Giggs standing out as a
stand-off, and his pace and skill so
impressed observers that he was due to
play a trial for Great Britain. The start
of his Old Trafford apprenticeship ruled
him out.

*He was an all-rounder, good enough to play
rugby for Lancashire and with a talent for
basketball. We are very proud of him.*
**Robert Mason, Giggs's former games
master at Moreside High School**

*Everybody thought he had great
potential, and the feeling was that
we had to keep hold of this lad.*
Dennis Schofield

LEGEND HAS IT that, at the age of 14,
Giggs was sitting at home with his mother
when Alex Ferguson came round peronally
to sign him as a Schoolboy. Giggs later
became a YTS trainee at the club earning
the princely sum of £29.50 a week. He
started playing for the A and B teams
at the weekend and trained with the squad
for a week during the school holidays. This
was alongside some of the most talented
players in the country, including Nicky
Barmby, a fellow team member of the
England Schoolboy team.

*I realised immediately that he could become
a top player. He had tremendous speed and
pace. He was an outstanding prospect.*
Eric Harrison, United Youth Team Coach

BY 1989 GIGGS had served as a successful captain of the England Under-15 Schoolboys' team where they had a triumphant record of seven victories from nine matches, including the scalps of England's bitterest foes West Germany, Holland, France and Belgium.

Though born in Wales, Giggs wasn't eligible to play for the national team as he wasn't attending a Welsh school, hence his playing instead for the English Schoolboys. On one occasion, his team beat Wales 5-0. However, Giggs was later to return to his roots and gain a regular place in the Welsh national side alongside such names as Ian Rush and Dean Saunders. As a result Giggs has often been described as 'the best player England never had'.

DUE TO HIS TALENT,
Giggs started playing in
the Manchester United
Youth team while still at
school, even though he
was two years younger
than most of the others.
As a result, he tasted
success early, playing in
three Youth Cup Finals in
a row. Although his team
lost their first two Finals,
when Giggs was made
captain of the side it was
a case of third time lucky
and United won the
trophy. By this stage,
Ryan was already playing
in United's reserves.

Ryan was very talented,
very confident, a terrific
lad and a pleasure to
work with.
Nobby Stiles

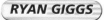
GETTING THE BREAK

DURING THE 1990-91 SEASON, Giggs spent most of his time training with the Reserves and Youth team. He'd barely played any matches with the Reserves before he got his call-up to the first team at the end of February. Named as a substitute for a midweek fixture against Sheffield United at Bramall Lane, Giggs merely watched from the bench.

On 2 March 1991, almost a week later, Giggs was again named as a sub for a match against Everton. Denis Irwin was injured in the first half and Giggs finally made his debut for United, in front of 44,000 people at Old Trafford. Playing up front alongside Lee Sharpe, who had just been awarded the PFA Young Player of the Year award, and Danny Wallace, Giggs had a lot to prove.

His pace, balance and control had identified him as a prodigy when he broke into the United first team as a 17-year-old in the spring of 1991.
Hugh McIlvanney, *The Sunday Times*, 1995

This wisp of a lad rides tackles with devastating speed and hypnotic balance. There is something remote about Giggs, remote in a face that looks old beyond its years.
Rob Hughes, *The Times*, **1991**

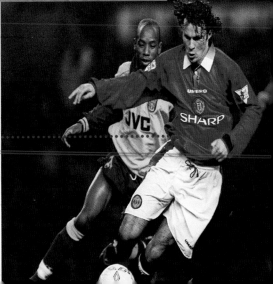

GIGGS'S DEBUT was well documented and though he only made one other appearance, two months later near the end of the season, it was one he could really cherish. Playing in the derby match away to Manchester City, Giggs scored the only goal of the match – United, once again, had beaten their old enemies and they had Giggs to thank.

He did not play any part in the rest of United's season as Alex Ferguson, 'the Boss', as Giggs always calls him, chose to rest and protect him from the media glare that he inevitably attracted. None of the young stars at United, like Lee Sharpe and Giggs, were allowed to talk to the press.

I am going to protect Ryan all I can.
Alex Ferguson

RYAN WAS GIVEN the chance to mature at his own pace without having to deal with all the pressures that have affected other players in the past. Naturally, actions like this did not make Alex Ferguson popular and he was constantly criticised by Des Lynam on *Match of the Day* for not letting journalists near his prodigies. However, this did not prevent journalists from writing about Giggs; for them, he was the nearest player to George Best they had ever seen.

Ryan Giggs is the most exciting footballing talent to emerge in British football since George Best.
People, 1994

Ryan Giggs is the best British footballer since George Best.
***The Star,** October 1994*

You want to be a footballer, not a celebrity. You get a microphone or camera in the face and you're not ready.
Ryan Giggs, talking to Jim White, *GQ*

GIGGS AND SHARPE started a trend at Old Trafford. After their arrival, Ferguson signed up more young trainees during the summer months of 1991: future England stars David Beckham, Gary Neville and Paul Scholes all joined the club. United were building for the future, a future in which Giggs was going to play a major part.

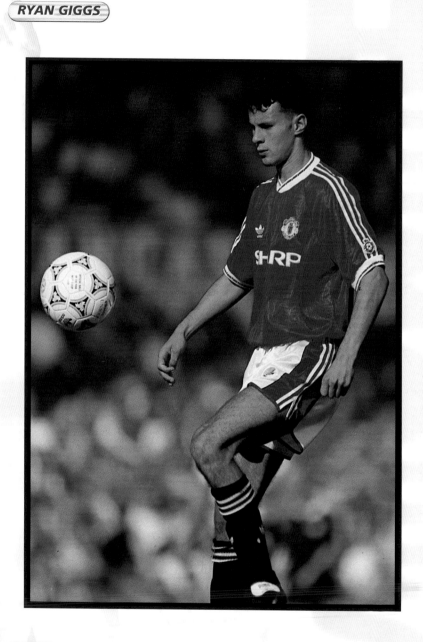

BY THE START of the next season, Giggs was ready and so were the fans. They had beaten Crystal Palace to win the 1990 FA Cup; this was followed by a good run in Europe in the Cup Winners' Cup. United reached the final in Rotterdam and beat Johann Cruyff's Barcelona 2-1. Now all Manchester United's fans were waiting for was for their team to win the League Championship; a feat they hadn't achieved since 1967. The 1991-92 season had begun.

Though Giggs was left out of the opening line-up for the first match of the season against Notts County, he was brought on in the second half to replace Darren Ferguson. After that he didn't look back. Lee Sharpe's thigh injuries meant that Giggs was called on to take his left-wing position – unfortunate for Sharpe but a bonus for Giggs.

It didn't take Giggs long to score for United. On 7 September 1991, he struck home his first goal of the season against Norwich City at Old Trafford. Giggs's season was really beginning as was United's battle for the title. Having signed Peter Schmeichel, arguably one of the best goalkeepers in the First Division, Paul Parker and Andrei Kanchelskis, they had a fierce start to the season; however, by the last few games of the season, United couldn't hold on. Eric Cantona and his Leeds team-mates pipped them to the post.

Giggs, however had one consolation that season – the Rumbelows Cup (as the League Cup used to be known): one of his most blistering performances in September 1991 was against Cambridge United in the first leg of the second round. He scored a goal after floating past the defenders and chipping his shot into the net.

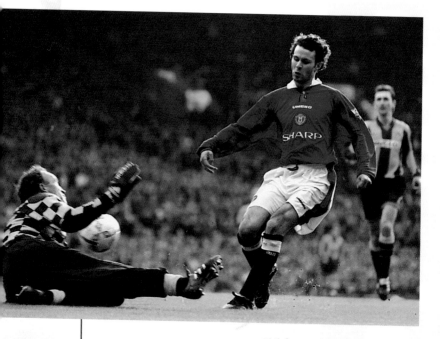

With one opponent at his elbow, another trailing him two yards away, he glided over the next 40 yards. He never glanced back and he touched the ball only once to maintain its momentum before, a stride inside the penalty area, he chipped the goalkeeper as if his left foot were a golfing iron.

Rob Hughes, *The Times*, 1991

THE RUMBELOWS CUP was all about Giggs. United may have made early exits from the FA and Cup Winners' Cups but they were still flying high in the League and the Rumbelows Cup. Manchester United reached the final and Giggs played a major part.

United had drawn in the first leg of their semi-final against Middlesbrough but, on the return leg held at Old Trafford, Giggs scored a winning goal. United had beaten Middlesbrough 2-1 and were on their way to Wembley! The Reds were playing a strong Nottingham Forest team – roused by their manager Brian Clough – but even the mighty Cloughie was powerless to stop a Giggs through-ball finding Brian McClair, who fired his goal into the net. United won the match 1-0 and Giggs and his team-mates ascended the famous Wembley steps to collect their medals. He was still only 18 years old.

LEEKS AND DRAGONS

GIGGS MAY HAVE BEEN INCREDIBLY disappointed at losing out on the Championship with United but there was one aspect of 1991 that eased the pain for him: his country needed him. That was the year he won his first cap of many for Wales.

Rumour has it that Terry Venables, the former England manager, was amazed that Giggs had been allowed to slip through their fingers and play for the Welsh. However, though he'd played as a Schoolboy for England, Giggs was born in Wales, his parents were Welsh – and as a Welshman that is the country he is ultimately eligible to play for.

He started off his Wales career some years earlier in an Under-18 match against England; it was played in front of a large Welsh support in Wrexham in the World Youth Cup in 1991. Giggs was playing against his former England Schoolboy team-mate Nicky Barmby. Giggs, however, was the name that everyone remembered because he was easily the best player on the pitch.

Fast on the wing, with tremendous pace and incredible accuracy, he was a nightmare for the young English defenders.

Ryan seems to float over the surface rather than run like the rest of us. So light on his feet and blessed with wonderful, wonderful balance. I can't stress that quality too much.
Alex Ferguson

The English team were frightened to death by Ryan.
Jimmy Shoulder, Director of Coaching for Wales

IT WAS SHORTLY after his time in the youth team that Giggs made his international debut against a fearsome German side, a team which included German legends Lothar Matthäus and Jürgen Klinsmann – alongside other famous internationals such as Doll and Effenberg. The match was Wales v West Germany in the qualifying rounds for the World Cup. Terry Yorath, Wales manager at the time, gave Giggs his golden chance to come on – in the 86th minute of the match. Though he only had about three touches of the ball against the powerful West German side everyone knew that Giggs's day had come.

When Ryan Giggs came on as a substitute for Wales against West Germany on 16 October 1991, he became the youngest ever man to play for Wales at the age of 17 years and 321 days.
Michael Crick

When I gave him his debut, it turned out that he was the youngest-ever player to appear for Wales, though that was not a record we planned to beat – it just happened that way, but it is a record he deserves.
Terry Yorath, former Wales manager

I can tell my grandchildren I played with Ryan Giggs.
Kevin Ratcliffe, former Everton and Wales international player

NEVERTHELESS, even with Ryan Giggs in their team, the Welsh were defeated by the West Germans. Frustratingly, both Giggs and Wales were denied the opportunity to show everyone what they were capable of on a world stage.

Some footballers would have crumbled under the tremendous pressure, especially at such a young age, but not Giggs. Surrounded by seasoned international players, like Mark Hughes, Ian Rush, Dean Saunders and goalkeeper Neville Southall, Giggs could grow as a player and learn from their experience.

Giggs spent the next year and a half coming on for Wales as a substitute, until he made his full debut, against Belgium, in front of a highly emotional Welsh crowd at Cardiff Arms Park stadium.

*I gave him his first start in the
return match [against Belgium]
and he was tremendous.*
Terry Yorath

ONCE AGAIN, Giggs showed
the world why he's a top-class
player. Against the tough
Belgian team, the Welsh were
finding it hard to get a break.
Then, they were awarded a
free-kick outside the box. Giggs
volunteered to take it and he
bent it over the wall, floating it
into the goal past the
unfortunate Belgian keeper –
an outstanding performance
from a true professional.

*You really see a difference in
the side when he's playing.
There's no doubt he has it
within him to become one of
the all-time greats.*
Mike Smith, former Wales manager

AFTER THEIR GLORIOUS win over Belgium, Wales were *so* close to playing in the World Cup – all that stood between them and it was Romania. By November 1993, it was up to Wales to beat their opposers by two clear goals and then they could travel to the USA alongside England, Scotland and Ireland for the World Cup. Unfortunately, they couldn't pull it off. The Romanians, with George Hagi, had their own agenda and though Dean Saunders scored, a missed penalty by the Welsh and two Raducioiu goals meant that, once again, the fans were denied the opportunity of seeing Giggs perform on a world stage.

The Euro 96 campaign saw the Welsh team given another opportunity to play in an international competition. They were drawn against Moldova, Bulgaria, Albania, Georgia and Germany. Giggs only played two matches in the qualifiers and saw his team lose 5-0 to Georgia, 3-2 to Moldova and later on 1-0 to Georgia. However, Giggs did score a goal, helping Wales record a 2-0 win over Albania.

He is one of the true talents, a player who would be in the team if you were picking a Great Britain side. He has awesome pace and, just as importantly, he is extremely perceptive.
Mike Smith

WALES ARE ALSO vying for a place in the 1998 World Cup in France, but, again, it looks as if this too might be impossible. At times like this the comparisons with George Best are rife. Both, arguably, the greatest talents of their generation and both missing out on the chance to dazzle and perform on international stages as Best's Northern Ireland team failed to qualify for major international competitions.

There's no way Ryan Giggs is another George Best. He's another Ryan Giggs.
Denis Law, former Manchester United player

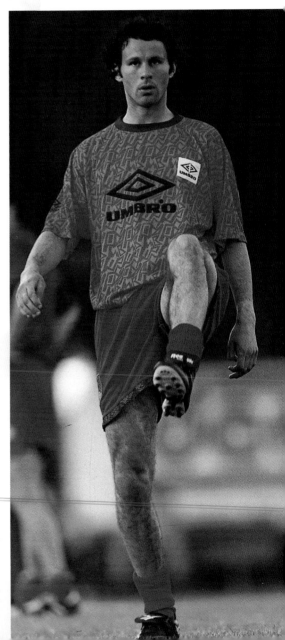

TRIUMPHING AT LAST

GIGGS

GIGGS HAD A LOT TO PROVE in the 1992-93 season – he had to live up to the expectations of the Old Trafford faithful. The summer before, he'd won his team-mate, Lee Sharpe's, title of PFA Young Player of the Year.

It was not much consolation for the Old Trafford faithful that, for the first time since the Busby era, the club's youth team proved themselves to be the best in the country. The team that won the FA Youth Cup included Neville, Beckham, Gillespie, Scholes, Butt and of course, Ryan Giggs.

He was ready for more. Maturing into a top-class player, he was leaving his youth team-mates behind. United had only just lost out to Leeds for the Championship title, in the previous season, and every supporter in the red half of Manchester was desperate to get their hands on the title.

However, United started the season poorly. They lost their first two matches and drew with Ipswich in the third. After narrowly beating Southampton away, Giggs and his United army travelled to Nottingham Forest only five days later. There was a proper Welsh onslaught as Mark Hughes opened the scoring and Giggs scored the winning goal: they beat Forest 2-0. The season was finally going his way.

Ryan Giggs, Ryan Giggs, running down the wing, Ryan Giggs, Ryan Giggs, running down the wing. Feared by the Blues, loved by the Reds, Ryan Giggs, Ryan Giggs, Ryan Giggs.
Old Trafford Chant

Ryan's second season was terrific.
Alex Ferguson

He helped me develop as a player and taught me how to deal with the pressures of being a professional footballer. He has to be one of the best managers of all time.
Ryan Giggs, on Alex Ferguson, Action Replay, October 1996

His skills are prodigious.
Neil Kinnock, Evening Standard, 1994

ON 19 SEPTEMBER,
United were playing
Tottenham at White Hart
Lane. In front of 33,296
supporters Giggs opened the
scoring on the half-time
whistle. What made this goal
really memorable was the
way Giggs, still only 18, stole
the ball, pushed it between a
defender's legs, dragged it
clear of the goalkeeper and
then threaded his shot into
the net from a difficult angle.

The adulation con-
tinued. Giggs appeared on
the opening titles of *Match
Of The Day*, scoring his goal
against Spurs that was so
incredible in its execution.
Then, he received the
ultimate accolade: they put
him on the opening titles of
Fantasy Football League. The
inimitable Giggs was shown
darting past a red-faced
defender displaying his
dazzling trickery.

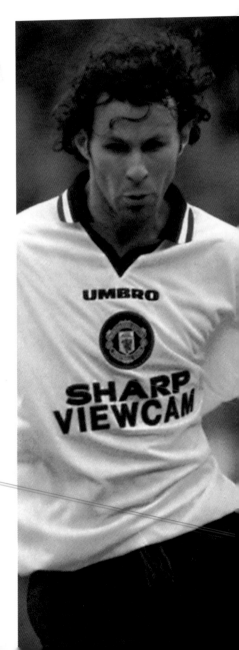

Giggs has tremendous quality. A great left foot, pace, crossing ability and finishing. But he also has another dimension – he's good when he hasn't got the ball. I worked with Ian Rush at Chester and at international level. Giggs reminds me of him in that he won't let people settle.

Doug Livermore, Spurs coach

Ryan's power and skill are due to his incredible balance. He can wrong-foot anybody just by a movement and when you think a tackler is going to get his foot to the ball, he seems to float or ride or roll over the challenge. The defender always seems to go down, while the lad stays on his feet.

Alex Ferguson

UNITED MADE a shrewd acquisition in November of 1992. Enter the King, Eric Cantona. He quickly fitted into the team, with deft passes that brought out the best in his colleagues. Giggs was one of those who benefited as the two of them built up a solid understanding during the season working closely with one another to help United to that elusive Championship title.

He puts defenders under pressure expecting him to make mistakes. It's a terrific asset.
Doug Livermore

It was a golden age of attacking football and United won their first League Championship in an agonising quarter of a century. They were top of the tree and Ryan Joseph Giggs was, naturally, the new George Best.
Total Sport, 1997

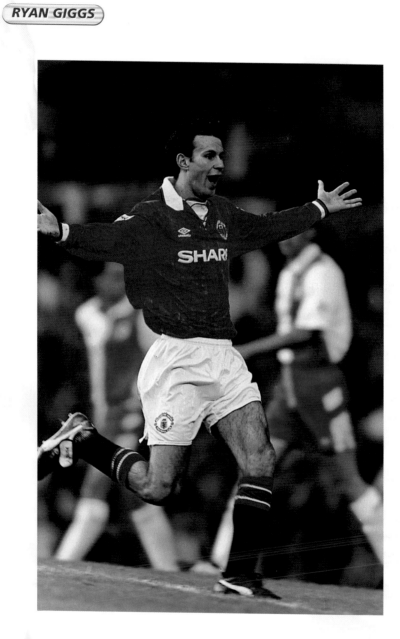

Everyone knew about the wizard on the wing.
Richard Kurt

WHEN SOUTHAMPTON faced Giggs in February, they saw the player in devastating form. The Saints had taken the lead but Giggs scored two superb goals in the space of two minutes to win the game for United. Vintage Giggs.

Speaking as a football fan, I thought he was brilliant. Speaking as a member of the goalkeepers' union, he's a nightmare.
Tim Flowers, Southampton goalkeeper

He [Giggs] has made himself the key man.
Chris Kamara, former Sheffield United player

He has such a wonderful attitude, such a desire to release the greatest that is within him and it's up to us at the club to assist his development. He is a thinker about the game and a listener, no question about that.
Alex Ferguson

Football is his mastermind subject. Football he loves. Which is just as well: he has, to all intents and purposes, been a full-time footballer since he was fourteen.
Jim White, *GQ*

BY THE BEGINNING of May, 1995, United already knew they had won the title. Aston Villa had to play Oldham on the Sunday before United's Monday clash with Blackburn. Oldham were involved in their own relegation dogfight and had to win to keep their challenge going. Oldham won, United had won the Championship.

In front of a crowd of 40,447 supporters, United were ready to party. However, Blackburn decided to make the newly crowned Champions work for their throne. Blackburn's flourish did not last long, as Giggs cancelled out Gallagher's strike in the 21st minute of the match.

Up strode Giggs to arrow a free-kick over a defensive wall and into the top corner of the net as if it had been tracked there by computer. That explosive strike won an approving nod from Michel Platini, the master of the art of free-kick taking, sitting as a guest in the director's box.
Frank Malley, journalist

Giggs's growing authority on the field had helped United to their first Championship in 26 years.
Jim White, GQ

DOUBLE JOY

THE START OF THE NEW SEASON for United saw them as defending champions, a title that they were anxious to keep hold of. They started their campaign well when Giggs scored his first goal on 15 August 1993 against Norwich City at Carrow Road.

It was not a vintage Giggs goal, but one that highlighted his skill as an expert goal poacher. A deflection from a Mark Hughes shot was punched away by Bryan Gunn but Giggs was there to push the ball over the line with his left foot in the 26th minute.

Only a week later, Ryan was on the ball again with a stunning free-kick against newly promoted Newcastle. It swerved past the Newcastle keeper, Pavel Srnicek – United took the lead 1-0.

It was the first of many such victories for the United team that season. In total, the side played 62 games, losing only six of them and winning 41. Furthermore, they had only conceded 55 goals compared to the 125 goals scored.

Giggs played his part in all this – he was the third highest goalscorer in the team with his 17 goals in total over the season, behind his Welsh team-mate Mark Hughes and the inspirational Eric Cantona. This season was one of Giggs's most successful with United as they carved their place in the history books.

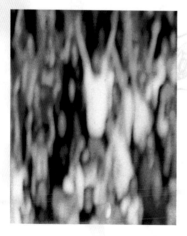

United will once again be the team to beat.
Daily Telegraph, 1993

Fergie's aces had treated themselves to a flyer with two impressive wins and looked to be heading for another when Ryan Giggs fired them into a first-half lead with another brilliant free kick.
Sunday Express, August 1993

GIGGS KNEW that he wanted to stay with Man United for some time, and by October 1993, a month before his 20th birthday, Giggs signed a new contract to keep him at Old Trafford for the next five years.

Ryan is a thinker about life. He'll watch people's behaviour and listen to what they are saying and analyse it all. It's a capacity which sets him apart from most other players.
Alex Ferguson

Whether breaking past an opponent from wide on the wing or erupting with dramatic suddenness through the middle of a defence, his runs are an exhilarating blend of grace and devastation. He has the attacking footballer's classic trinity of gifts: pace, control and balance. And the greatest of these is balance, since it so crucially underpoints the effectiveness of the other two.
Hugh McIlvanney, *Sunday Times*, December 1993

In football you've got to be quick and I always have been. I love that feeling of knocking a ball past a defender and going. Just as he thinks he will get his tackle in, you touch it a little bit more and you are away.
Ryan Giggs

AFTER GIGGS'S 20th birthday, he really took off. He scored two goals in the space of six minutes in the match against Oldham Athletic at Boundary Park. United won the match 5-0 and the team, bolstered by the skills of Eric Cantona, a new arrival that season, Andrei Kanchelskis and Giggs himself, knew that maybe this was going to be their season.

United played all three flying wingers in an awesome display of high speed fire-power. It was marvellous to watch, as long as you were not an Oldham fan.
The Daily Star, December 1993

THREE DAYS after the Oldham match, on 1 January, United had a tough match against the former champions, Leeds. Giggs, however, showed his mettle, engaging in a terrific battle for supremacy against the young Leeds defender Gary Kelly. United drew the match, but Giggs could be proud of his performance. It was the beginning of a new year. No one could ignore his vital contributions in each match, Giggs was better than ever.

Ryan Giggs redefined football geometry to keep Manchester United's eyes focused on their impossible dream ... Giggs had the tightest of angles to aim for but the Welshman knew exactly where the goal was.
Daily Express, 1994

Having also to cope with Ryan Giggs threading silken traces down the left, Charlton were unable to maintain the pressure.
Sunday Times, 1994

BY APRIL OF 1994, Giggs had already scored 10 goals and United were in the final of the FA Cup. After a tight match against their North-East opponents, Oldham and a 1-1 draw, after extra time, in the semi-final, Giggs joined his team-mates Denis Irwin, Andrei Kanchelskis and Eric Cantona to score a goal in their 4-1 victory. Giggs was on his way to the twin towers of Wembley.

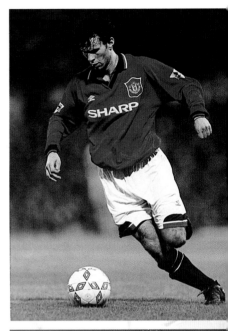

Getting to the final made up for United's disappointment at just missing out on winning the Coca-Cola Cup. Giggs had scored the only goal in their semi-final first leg win against Sheffield Wednesday, but, in the final against Aston Villa not even Giggs could prevent his team losing 3-1. However, United had more important things in hand, they were on their way to winning the Championship.

The wingers, Kanchelskis and Giggs, scored the goals in a victory that meant, no matter that Blackburn go doggedly on, Manchester United are now close to becoming the first team since Liverpool, ten years ago, to win the championship in successive seasons.
The Times, April 1994

... his cross was met by Giggs. It was the Welsh International's 17th goal of the season and took United's tally to an incredible 119 in all competitions.
The Sun, May 1994

BY THE END of May 1994, Giggs had two more awards to add to his, now growing, collection. United had achieved the first double in the club's history and Giggs had played a vital contributing role. So it was no surprise when he won the PFA Young Player of the Year award for the second year running.

FIRST INJURY

AT THE AGE OF 20, RYAN Giggs had already won two Championships, an FA Cup and a League Cup winners' medal: now it was time for the 1994-95 season to begin.

The pre-season training had gone well for Giggs and United. Travelling across Ireland, Giggs showed that he still had that magic touch – dancing around the pitch and speeding down the wing, it was business as usual.

Giggs scored against the Irish team Dundalk in front of 12,000 fans and then scored again against Shelbourne. Giggs-fever was evident at the match when, to the great amusement of the crowd, a young female fan ran on to the pitch in the Irish stadium to kiss him whilst he was preparing to take a corner. It did not put Giggs off his stride, United won the match 3-0.

After winning the Championships for two successive years, United were on a roll. They reminded people of Liverpool in the 1980s, a team which totally dominated the top flight and were almost unstoppable. Like Liverpool, United became the side to beat, or so everyone thought.

The Charity Shield against Blackburn Rovers boosted United's confidence just before the start of the season. At Wembley, in front of 60,402 fans, the Reds beat their opposition 2-0. Giggs did not score a goal on this occasion but was still in the thick of the action.

*The corner flew in from Giggs's boot
and Cantona back-headed into the
box. Waiting with an acrobatic finish
was Ince.*
The Sun, 1994

AS IT TURNED out, both the club
and Giggs did not pull off the top
performances that everyone had
come to expect from them. Giggs
only scored one goal in the League,
in their 3-1 victory over Wimbledon
in August of that year, a goal in
their Cup run, during January when
the Reds beat Wrexham 5-2 and two
goals against IFK Gothenburg in the
first round of the UEFA Champions'
League.

*In 1968, it was the stunning ability
of George Best that powered United
to glory in this competition. Twenty-
six years later, Giggs looks
determined to take the European
stage by storm.*
Daily Star, 1994

*If I had to chose an all-time United
team, Giggs would be in it. And he'd
be wearing Reebok boots.*
Bobby Charlton, Reebok television commercial

GIGGS'S performances were also not helped by the fact that he picked the first major injury of his career. His original injury occurred during a match against Ipswich at the start of the season when he got a calf strain, and then he developed problems with his ankle, Achilles tendon and hamstring – all on the same leg. This meant that Ryan not only missed vital matches, but training sessions too.

Nevertheless, when you have Giggs playing for your team, whether fully healthy or not, he is still one of the most talented wingers in the country and that counts for a lot.

I did play a few games when I didn't feel my best. There was one game where I'd been ill the day before, and I managed to score.
Ryan Giggs, *You* magazine, 1994

RYAN RECEIVED a lot of media attention during 1994 as his autobiography *My Story* was published. It was a measure of his popularity that it remained a best-seller for several weeks. Author Stephen F. Kelly claimed that Ryan was now the most talked-about player in the game.

Meanwhile, Giggs looked to have put his injuries behind him and appeared to be back on form by the New Year. In United's match against Blackburn Rovers at the end of the month, a back-to-form Giggs executed a perfect cross to Eric Cantona who headed the ball past the unfortunate Tim Flowers in the 80th minute.

United, missing both Giggs and Eric Cantona, after his controversial sending off against Crystal Palace, could not maintain their hold on the Premiership. United missed out winning the Premiership title for a record third time. However, Giggs still received a lot of media attention. Injured or not, he was still a class player whom no one could ignore.

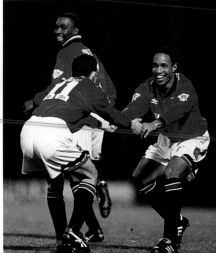

The one shaft of unpredictable light on the pitch was Giggs.
Richard Kurt

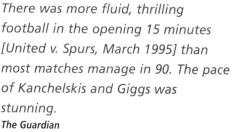

There was more fluid, thrilling football in the opening 15 minutes [United v. Spurs, March 1995] than most matches manage in 90. The pace of Kanchelskis and Giggs was stunning.
The Guardian

What a great young player. Giggs is definitely the best prospect I have ever seen.
Alex Ferguson, *Action Replay*, **October 1996**

GIGGS HAD flashes of genius but, due to the injury he'd picked up earlier in the season, was not able to play a constant part in United's Championship and FA Cup campaign.

The end of the season was looming and Giggs had only played a few matches before the FA Cup final against Everton. Alex Ferguson was reluctant to play Giggs for the whole match, so he came on as a substitute in the second half. In front of a filled Wembley Stadium, there were 79,592 fans in the ground, Giggs performed some of his Welsh wizardry.

It is arguable that he could have won us the League at the death. He nearly turned the Cup final around for us when we brought him on as a substitute.
Alex Ferguson

It's five years since we've won nothing. Sometimes our players forget what defeat is like. They know now.
Alex Ferguson

UNITED MISSED out on both the Championship and FA Cup this season but Giggs was recovering well from his injuries and was ready to face the challenges of the new season.

All I think about at the moment is winning trophies and being successful with Manchester United.
Ryan Giggs

COMING BACK

MANCHESTER UNITED UNDERWENT some changes during the close season. Ferguson had sold Paul Ince, Mark Hughes and Andrei Kanchelskis and some fans felt that United's time at the top was over. However, the 1995-96 season saw United winning another double and another vintage season for Giggs.

After United's disappointment the previous season, they knew that they had to do something dramatic and prove that they would not choke on the big occasion. Initially, it looked bad for the former champions, by mid-season, Newcastle United had a 12-point lead. But, United had more fighting experience: they'd had disappointments during the 1991-92 and 1994-95 seasons when they'd let the championship slip through their fingers – they weren't about to let that happen again.

United's season did not start off as well as expected. Their first match of the season saw them lose 3-1 at Aston Villa. Giggs, however, could not be blamed, he was still slightly injured. The match was later followed by a 3-0 defeat by Second Division York City which disappointed their fans.

Giggs, playing his first full game of the season, was majestic. His pace, vision and close control mesmerised the Russians.
Daily Star, 1995

AFTER A CONFIDENCE-BOOSTING performance in Europe against the Russian side Rotor Volgograd – Giggs did not score but performed with valour – he went and scored a superb equaliser against Everton at Goodison Park to aid his team in their domestic campaign. He blasted a shot past his Welsh compatriot, goalkeeper Neville Southall, in the 74th minute. The fans could relax – United were not going to blow it again.

RYAN GIGGS

He's a class player.
Alex Ferguson

GIGGS PLAYED a vital role in the team's double double success. Supplying players with accurate crosses, sharp corners and blistering free kicks. His injury was well behind him, Old Trafford's prodigal son had returned.

Match winner Ryan Giggs ended his Premiership hell to shoot Manchester United to the top of the table ... Giggs, without a League goal for a year, replaced Paul Scholes and broke his duck with a classy left-footer.
People, 1995

Whether playing in midfield, on the wing or up front he appears to have matured into a thinking footballer who is in complete control of himself. Suddenly there is more variety to his game, he's putting his foot on the ball and displaying a greater repertoire of passing, perhaps brought about by his new midfield role. Giggs is shaking off the shackles of the hundred-mile-an-hour English game and Manchester United and supporters everywhere will be the beneficiaries.
The Observer, 1995

*Footballers who can electrify a crowd have become an
endangered species in Britain and the welcome importation
of such players from overseas can never stifle the longing for
home-bred deliverers of old magic. Giggs feeds that need,
and pleasure over his current brilliance is deepened by a sense
of reclaiming a treasure that many thought was lost.*
Hugh McIlvanney, *The Sunday Times*, 1995

*Giggs is 22 next month, long in the tooth for a teeny idol, but
maturing as a man and a player into such a revelation it can
only be a matter of time before Italian bloodsuckers start
pestering United again.*
Daily Mail, 1995

GIGGS KEPT himself injury-free for the whole of the season and, after Eric Cantona's return from suspension, the two players built a relationship that was almost telepathic in its brilliance. Ryan, all the critics agreed, had matured.

By November, he showed the world that he was over the injury nightmares when Giggs scored the third quickest goal in Premiership history. Playing against Southampton, Paul Scholes passed to Cantona who laid it to Giggs's feet and then with startling precision the ball was in the net. The match was only 15 seconds old.

On this form Giggs, scintillating in a new, free-ranging, attacking midfield role, will become one of the dominant players in this season's Championship chase.
Sunday Express, November 1995

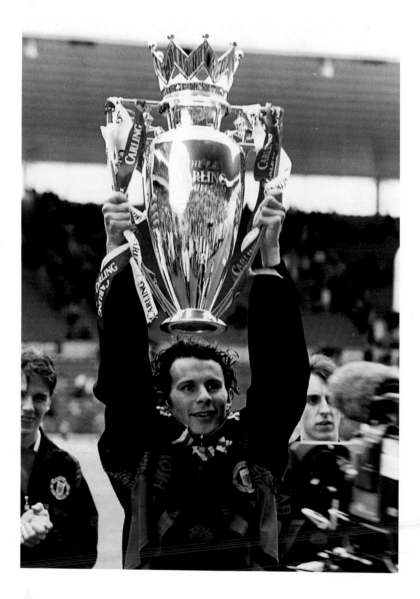

He is back to the way we know he can play and he's full of confidence.
Alex Ferguson

The only problem with Giggs is that he doesn't have a German passport.
Berti Vogts, Germany manager

With Ryan Giggs providing the inspiration through his sheer genius, this encounter [Coventry 0 - United 4] became increasingly one-sided.
Daily Mirror, November 1995

Ryan Giggs bewitched the City Ground last night.
The Guardian, November 1995

Giggs – tutored by Ferguson, the shrewdest of managers – has fulfilled his promise. Giggs could always dribble and outpace defenders. Now his passing and tackling are sharper, and Ferguson has improved this natural left-footer's ability to pass with his right foot.
Financial Times, 1996

NOW 22, he had become totally unselfish in the goal mouth. Passing up the opportunity of a half-chance, he would find an unmarked attacker with an incisive pass making their job easy – all they had to do was tap the goal and United would collect the points.

United spent the next few months chasing Newcastle for the Premiership title and it was not until March that United edged in front, though at this stage the Toon army still had two games in hand. By April, the battle for the top had intensified but in a local derby against relegation strugglers Manchester City, Giggs was on hand, once again, to score the winning goal in the 77th minute.

Gone are many of the tricks that baffled defenders but often produced no results. Instead, he has concentrated on the basics, passing and crossing, to calamitous effect for opposing defences.
Mail on Sunday, 1996

BY MAY, United had the double in their sights. Newcastle were slipping up and on 5 May 1996, Newcastle had to beat Tottenham and United had to lose to Middlesbrough. The Reds won 3-0 and the last goal of the winning Champions was struck by none other than Ryan Giggs – a fitting end to a tremendous season.

Ryan Giggs completed another day of triumph for Ferguson with another memorable goal.
The Guardian, 1996

UNITED ENDED the season
beating Liverpool at Wembley in
the FA Cup in front of 79,007 fans.
Yet another winning medal for
Giggs to add to his vast collection.

THE FUTURE

UNITED HAD ANOTHER STORMING season during 1996-97. Winning the championship, again, Giggs played another vital role. The spotlight was beginning to move away from him and over to the other young prodigies that Alex Ferguson was nurturing. David Beckham, Gary Neville, Phil Neville, Nicky Butt and Paul Scholes, though all members of the same youth team as Giggs were now regulars and blossoming in the first team.

Giggs, though only 23, was seen as a father figure. He was one of the best people to advise the young team-mates as he had done all this before. He'd been under intense scrutiny and had come through it – injuries and all.

Giggs started the season with a slight injury, but as he's such a versatile player, Alex Ferguson decided to play him up front – Ryan's pace meant that he could race down the middle of the pitch and still continue to flummox defenders.

Meanwhile, United were fleshing out their team. Alex Ferguson bought five new players, who all promised much: Karel Poborsky, a familiar face from Euro 96, Jordi Cruyff, Ole Gunner Solskjaer, Ronny Johnsen and goalkeeper Rai Van Der Gouw. All of these were welcome additions in the team for Giggs as he now had more people to help him be even more creative.

It's incredible. Ryan Giggs has already been a wonderkid, a has-been, a superstar and a tabloid celebrity. He's won three championships and two doubles. And he is just 23.
Total Sport

It was breathless stuff and there was little hint of the stunning response from Everton as United's ploy to let Ryan Giggs tear into their defence left them ragged.
Manchester Evening News (United v. Everton, 21 August 1996)

GIGGS SUFFERED another injury last season, this time to his calf, and with United struggling slightly to find consistent form, he still managed to play in United's match against Arsenal in November. It was the first full match he had played in for two months.

Manchester United are looking like a class act again. How thoroughly fitting, then, that it should be Ryan Giggs, that epitome of physical equilibrium, whose return from injury helped end United's impersonation of a child's bike with a stabiliser missing.
The Telegraph

IN THE CHAMPIONS' LEAGUE, United were beaten at home by the Italian Champions, Juventus. This was the first time that the Reds had been beaten at home in a European match for 40 years.

However, they could draw some comfort from the fact that Giggs had an incredible second-half performance. At last, he proved his talent and pedigree on a European stage. He whizzed past the Italian defence, chipping in crosses for Cantona and succeeded in totally frustrating the Italian goalkeeper Angelo Peruzzi.

I want to win the European Cup with United.
Ryan Giggs

With his speed, balance and caressing touch, Giggs will always be a supremely gifted individualist.
Simon O'Hagan, journalist

THE CHAMPIONS' LEAGUE was slowly becoming Giggs's tournament. Looking like veterans, Giggs and Eric Cantona made a fantastic goal, when they were playing away to SK Rapid Wien: they worked together, passing to one another after Giggs had started the move from the half-way line. Giggs had scored in Europe, and the Austrians could not do a thing as United won 2-0.

Watching Giggs slide in with an angled tackle, cobra-like in its execution, the Beardsley association becomes so clear.
The Daily Telegraph

BY THE END of January 1997, United were top of the Premiership again and although Giggs had not played in all their League matches, no one can deny the impact he made when he did play.
His goalscoring was not as consistent as the previous season but away to Coventry in the middle of January he scored United's opening goal in the 60th minute – with his right foot. Then, just over a week later, Giggs scored another goal at home to Wimbledon, looping the ball from the near-post past a disgruntled Neil Sullivan.

We've had cases of the opposition doubling up on him, man-marking him, overloading on one side so he can't get the service – there are all kinds of obstacles a young forward has to overcome early in his career.
Alex Ferguson

IN MARCH, Ryan Giggs produced one of his best performances to date against the Portuguese Champions, FC Porto. With a display of breathtaking quality football, Giggs and his United team-mates played Porto off the park, down the coast and into the Mediterranean. Even the Porto fans' taunts of 'Liverpool' didn't put United off their stride. They beat them both.

United they attacked. Ryan Giggs and Eric Cantona conjuring pass after precision pass to embarrass the pride of Portugal.
The Daily Telegraph

At the heart of United's success lay an inspired performance by Giggs, with Beckham, his partner in midfield, not far behind.
The Guardian

RYAN HAS a dazzling future in front of him. People tend to forget that he's still under 25. Now, he's won four League titles, two FA Cups and a League Cup.

Meanwhile, Giggs is content just to get on to his beloved Old Trafford pitch and do what he does best – play football and listen to the praise come rolling in, whether he wants it or not.

Seeing the atmosphere here and how big a game it is I'd love to be involved in it next year.
Ryan Giggs, at the Champions' League Final, Rome, *90 Minutes*, 8 June 1996

He's got freedom. He's got the whole pitch to experiment. He's showing a whole array of talent – passing and dribbling.
Gordon Strachan

Giggs is blossoming to real greatness.
Daily Mail

He can pass, he can hold it, he can play one-twos and he is brave. Fortunately, too, he is intelligent.
Alex Ferguson

Giggs does things for his team that nobody else in the game can match.
George Best

FACT FILE

- *Full Name:*
  Ryan Joseph Giggs (born Ryan Joseph Wilson)
- *Height:*
  5'11"
- *Weight:*
  10st 9lb
- *Born:*
  29 November 1973 in Cardiff, Wales.
- *Career:*
  Played for **Manchester City's** Junior team under the name Ryan Wilson (changed to Giggs, his mother's maiden name, when his parents divorced).
  Manchester United
  From a Schoolboy, Giggs became a Trainee with United. Finally joined as a Pro in 1990.
  Honours with Man United: ESC 91; FAYC 92; FLC 92; PL 93, 94, 96; CS 93, 94; FAC 94, 96.
- *Position:* left wing.

RYAN'S GOLDEN MOMENTS

- *1981*
  Ryan is spotted playing football in his school team – Grosvenor Road Primary School, Swinton – by Dennis Schofield, a scout for Manchester City.
- *1983*
  After a couple of years of training, Dennis Schofield recommends Giggs to Dean's in Salford (a youth football club).

- *1985*
  Giggs starts training at Manchester City's Centre of Excellence – but his loyalty to United is apparent through his wearing of the forbidden red shirt while training.

- *1987*
  Salford Juniors Under-16 team make it to the national final v St Helens. The match is played at Old Trafford. His team lose, but Giggs is given his first taste of playing at Manchester United's home ground.

- *1987*
  Ryan and his mother are sitting at home when Alex Ferguson, manager of Manchester United, appears on the doorstep. Giggs is signed up as a Schoolboy.

- *1989*
  Giggs's England Under-15 Schoolboys, of which he is captain, have notched up a total of 7 victories in 9 games.

- *29 November 1990*
  Giggs signs to Manchester United as a Pro – on his 17th birthday.

- *2 March 1991*
  Ryan makes his first team debut, as a sub, against Everton. He plays in front of 44,000 fans at Old Trafford.

- *October 1993*
  Giggs signs a new contract to keep him at Old Trafford for the next five years.

- *1994 Charity Shield*
  United beat Blackburn Rovers 2-0 at Wembley. The crowd numbers 60,402 fans.

- *12 October 1996*
  Giggs is one of the United team who beat arch-rivals Liverpool in the last few minutes of the match.

GIGGSY'S GOALS

- Aged 17, Giggs makes his full debut in a 1-0 win over City. His is the only goal.
- On 7 September 1991, Ryan shoots home the first goal of the season, in a match against Norwich City at Old Trafford.
- In the latter end of September 1991, Giggs scores a spectacular goal versus Cambridge United, in the first leg of the second round of the Rumbelows Cup (now called the League Cup).
- In the semi-final of the 1991 Rumbelows Cup, United's winning goal is scored by Giggs! Ryan's top form sees Middlesbrough routed 2-1 and United on their way to Wembley.
- The 1991 final of the Rumbelows Cup sees an 18-year-old Ryan on cracking form again – his through ball to Brian McClair clinches the 1-0 victory over Nottingham Forest.
- During the 1992-93 season, Giggs notches up a total of 40 League goals.
- On 19 September 1993, Giggs scores the opening goal in United v Tottenham Hotspur at White Hart Lane. He is shown on the opening titles of *Match Of The Day* and on the opening titles of *Fantasy Football League*.
- Ryan is the third highest goalscorer on the team, coming behind the greats Eric Cantona and Mark Hughes.

- *April 1994*
Ryan has already scored 10 goals in the season so far!
- *August 1994*
Giggs scores once in United's 3-1 defeat of Wimbledon.
- On 18 November 1995, Manchester United beat Southampton 4-1 – Giggsy scores in the first 15 seconds of the match. His goal is the third quickest in Premiership history.
- On 5 May 1996, the last goal of the winning Champions League is kicked by Ryan Giggs.

INJURIES

- During the 1994-95 season, Giggs suffers the first major injury of his career. Playing in a match against Ipswich he strains his calf, and then develops problems with his ankle, Achilles tendon and hamstring – all on the same leg. As a result, Ryan misses several important matches and training sessions.
- Ryan starts the 1996-97 season with a slight strain injury, but continues to play.
- In August 1996, Giggs suffers a second injury so far this season. This one is more serious, a calf injury, and puts him out of action until November of the same year.

INTERNATIONAL GIGGS

- Although born in Wales, Giggs plays for the England Schoolboys – due to being at school in Manchester.
- As an adult, Ryan is snapped up by the land of his birth and becomes a regular for Wales.
- On 16 October 1991 Giggs gains his first Welsh cap when he plays as a sub against Germany, coming on in the 86th minute of the match. This match sees Ryan enter the record books as the youngest ever player to appear for Wales – since the side was founded in 1876. He is aged 17 years and 321 days.

HONOURS WON
- 1991 European Super Cup winner
- 1992 League Cup winner
- 1992 FA Youth Cup winner for United's Youth team (at the same time, Ryan is also playing in United's first team).
- 1993 PFA Young Player of the Year
- 1993 FA Premier League winner
- 1993 FA Charity Shield winner
- 1994 PFA Young Player of the Year
- 1994 FA Premier League winner
- 1994 FA Cup winner
- 1994 FA Charity Shield winner
- 1996 FA Premier League winner
- 1996 FA Cup winner
- 1996 FA Charity Shield winner
- 1997 FA Premier League winner
- 1997 FA Charity Shield winner

RUNNERS-UP HONOURS
- 1992 Football League Division One runner-up
- 1994 League Cup runner-up
- 1995 FA Premier League runner-up
- 1995 FA Cup runner-up

AWARDS FOR RYAN
- 1992 Barclays Bank Young Eagle of the Year
- 1992 PFA Young Player of the Year
- 1993 PFA Young Player of the Year
- Ryan made history by becoming the first player to win the PFA award in two consecutive years.
- Giggs came sixth in the 1993 World Footballer of the Year awards voted on by readers of *World Soccer* magazine.
- 1995-96 Ryan was chosen from approximately 50 nominees, as part of the Rothmans' Team of the Season in the Rothmans' Football Honours. The players are chosen by representatives of the Football Writers' Association: to be eligible, they have to have appeared in FA Carling Premiership matches during the season.

HIGH POINTS

- 19 full caps.
- Appeared as a sub in the 1991 European Super Cup Final.
- By the end of the 1996-97 season, Ryan Giggs had notched up a total of 250 goals.
- On a typical week Ryan's fan mail numbers 2000 letters.

MANCHESTER UNITED

- Ground: Old Trafford, Sir Matt Busby Way, Manchester M16 0RA.
- Ground capacity: 56,387.
- Pitch measurements: 116 yd x 76 yd.
- Year formed: 1878.
- Previous name: Newton Heath LYR.
- Nicknames: 'The Reds' or 'Red Devils'.
- Greatest score: 26 September 1956, Manchester United beat RSC Anderlecht 10-0 in the European Cup.
- Due to damage suffered by Old Trafford in the Second World War, the club took to playing home games at nearby Maine Road for several years.
- In 1957, United became the first English club to play in Europe. They reached the semi-finals of the European Cup; a performance to be repeated in 1958.
- Over two seasons (1956-57, Division One & 1958-59, Division One) United scored two identical totals of their record number of League goals – 103 goals, twice!

- 1958 saw disaster strike United, when eight players were tragically killed in the Munich Air disaster. Top star Bobby Charlton was among the survivors.
- Winners of the European Cup in 1968 – defeating Benfica 4-1 at Wembley.
- The most capped player in Manchester United's history is Bobby Charlton with 106 caps (England).
- United were the winners of the European Cup Winners' Cup in 1991.

- In 1934, United wore a surprise kit, sporting cherry and white hoops instead of their usual red shirts – for the first and only time. They were playing Millwall and won 2-0. After the match, the Reds resumed their normal kit.
- Ryan Giggs wears the No. 11 shirt – it was previously worn by his hero and football guru George Best. Giggs has spent a large part of his career being compared to Best.
- The record transfer fee ever paid by Manchester United was the £6,250,000 given to Newcastle United for fans' favourite Andy Cole. The transfer took place in January 1995.
- The largest transfer fee ever paid to United was in June 1995 when Internazionale bought Paul Ince for £7 million.
- Between 1956 and 1973, Bobby Charlton appeared 606 times for United. During these 17 years he scored 199 goals.
- In 1994, United became the fourth team this century to win the double (League and FA Cups). In 1996, they went down in sporting history by being the only team to win the double again.
- Ole Gunnar Solskjaer was the unexpected hero of United's 1996-97 season, notching up a total of 19 goals.
- On 12 October 1996, Manchester United played Liverpool at Old Trafford. 55,128 fans turned out – the largest crowd the ground had seen for 12 years.

Introduction and main text by Alex Wilkins.
Alex Wilkins started her career at the *Los Angeles Village View* newspaper, writing sports articles and book reviews. She was also a writer for the San Francisco arts magazine *Dafka* before moving to England in 1996. Alex now works as a freelance journalist, specialising in football. She is a staunch Man United supporter and has written for various club fanzines and *FourFourTwo*.

The Foundry would like to thank Helen Burke, Helen Courtney, Helen Johnson, Lucinda Hawksley, Lee Matthews, Morse Modaberi and Sonya Newland for all their work on this project.

Picture Credits
All pictures © copyright Empics Sports Photo Agency